T0285919

WHAT I WISH I KNEW
BEFORE BECOMING A
LEADER

A LEADER'S MANUAL

EARL A WILSON

ISBN 979-8-35096-537-7 eBook 979-8-35096-538-4

A Journey of Transformation and Inspiration

This book is more than just a collection of words and experiences; it's a testament to a transformative journey that has reshaped my life and, I hope, will touch yours too. As I penned down these pages, I delved deep into the reservoir of my life's experiences, each one a stepping stone that led me to where I stand today. My journey began with a bold leap - leaving the familiar shores of St. Vincent and the Grenadines to embrace a new career in a foreign land. This leap was not just geographical; it was a leap of faith, a venture into the unknown, stepping out of my comfort zone into a world that was culturally alien and challenging.

My career as a nurse was more than a profession; it was the crucible where my leadership was forged. In the corridors of healthcare, amidst the challenges of patient care, I learned the profound lesson of serving before leading. Little did I know, those early days were laying the groundwork for my leadership path.

This book is a mosaic of my life's errors and triumphs, each mistake a lesson, each success a pearl of wisdom. It's a journey that I now share with you, hoping that it lights your path and inspires you to carve your own trail of leadership.

I dedicate this book to God who has guided me, to my loving family - my wife Desiree, my mother Veronica, and my children Ashlee, Renee, De'Andre', Ayden, Akira, and Adashea, who have been my unwavering support. To my mentors, Diane and Kayce, who have been the lighthouses in my professional voyage, I owe a debt of gratitude.

As you turn these pages, remember that leadership is not confined to titles or industries; it's a universal language that resonates across all walks of life. The stories and principles in this book, drawn from various disciplines, are shared under the veil of anonymity to respect the privacy of the individuals and organizations involved.

Reflecting on my roots, I often think about my childhood in a neighborhood shadowed by adversity. Many of my friends from those days remain trapped in the same cycle of despair. Yet, whenever I return, I see a glimmer of pride in their eyes - a silent acknowledgment that if one of us succeeds, it's a victory for us all. This realization is a poignant reminder of the power of leadership and inspiration, even in the most unlikely places.

This book is not just my story; it's a canvas for you to paint your leadership journey. May these lessons guide you, inspire you, and ignite in you the courage to share your story, to "pave it forward" for others. Remember, every leader's journey starts with a single step, a step towards change, towards inspiring others, and towards creating a legacy that transcends boundaries and time.

FORWARD

The Quintessential Guide
for Every Leader

To the aspiring, emerging, and established leaders who hold this book in their hands,

Welcome to a journey that transcends the conventional boundaries of leadership literature. This book is not just a collection of chapters; it is a mosaic of wisdom, experiences, and insights that every leader should know, remember, and learn.

Leadership is an art as much as it is a science. It is a dance between the tangible and the intangible, between action and introspection, between leading and following. This book is crafted to guide you through these intricate dynamics, offering a compass to navigate the ever-evolving landscape of leadership.

As you embark on this journey, here are key tenets that this book will illuminate:

The Power of Authenticity: Leadership is not about wearing a mask of authority; it's about being true to yourself and those you lead. This book underscores the importance of authenticity, encouraging you to lead with your values and beliefs.

The Essence of Connection: You will learn that leadership is deeply rooted in the connections you forge – with your team, your peers, and yourself. Understanding and nurturing these connections are pivotal to effective leadership.

The Balance of Empathy and Decision-Making: Discover how to blend empathy with decisive action. This book teaches you how to listen with an open heart and lead with a firm hand, a balance that is crucial in today's dynamic leadership scenarios.

The Art of Going Beyond: Leadership is not confined to job descriptions or titles. You will learn the art of going the extra mile – not out of obligation, but driven by a genuine desire to make a difference.

The Journey of Continuous Learning: Leadership is a journey, not a destination. This book is a testament to the continuous learning and growth that leadership demands and encourages.

The Vision of Inclusivity: Embrace a leadership style that values diverse perspectives and fosters inclusivity. This book highlights the strength that lies in diversity and the importance of creating a space where every voice is heard.

The Challenge of Balancing Realism and Idealism: Learn to navigate the tightrope between aspirational goals and practical realities, a skill essential for any leader in any field.

The Importance of Work-Life Harmony: Understand the significance of balancing professional responsibilities with personal life, and how this balance can lead to a more fulfilling leadership experience.

As you turn each page, remember that leadership is as much about influencing others as it is about understanding yourself. This book is a mirror reflecting your potential, a guide to help you harness it, and a companion on your journey to effective and impactful leadership.

May the lessons within these pages inspire you, challenge you, and guide you as you carve your path in the world of leadership. Here's to your journey of becoming a leader who not only leads with the mind but also with the heart.

With best wishes on your leadership journey,

Earl CA Wilson
Your Guide and Companion on the Path of Leadership

Download: **PDF Workbook**

https://drive.google.com/
file/d/1NhmLUrx4j_LfvP5uUNQHXEpK5K9LHHUc/view?usp=sharing

CHAPTER 1

Building a Team, Not Just Friends

"True leadership means setting boundaries that foster respect and productivity, ensuring that professional camaraderie serves as the backbone of a high-performing team."

In the realm of leadership, the establishment and maintenance of professional boundaries are crucial for several reasons. First and foremost, these boundaries help in delineating the roles and responsibilities between a leader and their team members. This clarity is essential for maintaining respect, authority, and a functional hierarchy within an organization. Furthermore, professional boundaries prevent conflicts of interest and ensure that decisions are made based on merit and organizational needs, rather than personal relationships.

Leaders who fail to establish these boundaries might find themselves in challenging situations where their authority is undermined, or they are unable to enforce rules and expectations fairly. This can lead to a decrease in overall team performance, morale, and respect for leadership. Moreover, without clear boundaries, leaders may struggle to balance their personal and professional lives, leading to burnout and decreased effectiveness.

Personal Anecdote: The Challenge of Transitioning from Friend to Leader

My journey into the nuances of leadership and the importance of professional boundaries began when I was promoted to a leadership position within my team. Prior to my promotion, I had cultivated friendly relationships with my colleagues, including key influential staff members. We shared good times, often going out for drinks and socializing outside of work. This camaraderie, I believed, would be an asset in my new role.

However, the transition from being a peer to a leader brought unforeseen challenges. My attempts to win support through continued friendly engagements backfired. The same colleagues who had shared laughs and drinks with me began to see our personal relationship as a gateway to professional leniency. They started seeking favors, looking for ways to bypass deadlines, and expecting preferential treatment, assuming our friendship would override professional expectations.

The most significant challenge arose with a colleague who was a close friend before my promotion. This shift in our professional dynamic was difficult for both of us. I found myself in a delicate situation, needing to establish my authority and set boundaries without alienating someone I genuinely cared about. It was a tightrope walk between maintaining our friendship and asserting my new role as their leader.

This experience taught me a valuable lesson about the importance of professional boundaries in leadership. It highlighted the need to redefine relationships when moving into a leadership position, even if it means having uncomfortable conversations. Establishing clear boundaries early on is crucial to prevent misunderstandings and to maintain respect and authority as a leader. It's a balancing act of being approachable yet firm, friendly yet impartial, ensuring that professional responsibilities are never overshadowed by personal relationships.

ANECDOTE 1: THE BANKER'S DILEMMA

The Importance of Professional Boundaries

In the bustling financial district of a major city, there was a banker named Thomas. He was known for his sharp mind and charismatic personality. Thomas had recently been promoted to a managerial position at his bank, a role that he had worked tirelessly to achieve. Among his team were several colleagues who had become close friends over the years. They shared lunches, weekend outings, and family events. This close-knit group was a source of strength for Thomas, but it soon became his greatest challenge.

The Blurred Lines

Thomas's first few months as a manager were smooth sailing. His friends on the team were supportive, and their personal bond seemed to make the team more cohesive. However, as time passed, the dynamics began to shift. His friends started to take liberties, assuming that their personal relationship with Thomas would grant them certain privileges. Deadlines started to be treated with a casualness that wasn't afforded to other team members. They would often bypass formal channels, seeking Thomas's approval in informal settings, like during their lunch outings.

The Impact on Team Dynamics

This behavior did not go unnoticed by the rest of the team. A sense of unfairness began to brew. Non-friend team members felt marginalized and believed that Thomas's friends were receiving preferential treatment. This perception led to a decline in overall team morale. The informal decision-making process started to undermine the structured, merit-based approach that had governed the team's operations.

The Decision-Making Dilemma

Thomas found himself in a difficult position when it came to making critical decisions. His judgment was clouded by personal biases towards his friends. He started to second-guess his decisions, wondering if he was being too lenient with his friends or too harsh with others. This internal conflict not only affected his decision-making but also began to erode his confidence as a leader.

The Turning Point

The situation reached a tipping point when a crucial project deadline was missed due to laxity on the part of one of his friends. This incident was a wake-up call for Thomas. He realized that his failure to set and enforce professional boundaries had put the team's performance and his credibility at risk.

The Resolution

Thomas decided to take corrective action. He held a team meeting where he openly acknowledged the issue and reassured the team that going forward, professional standards would be uniformly applied, regardless of personal relationships. He had one-on-one conversations with his friends, explaining the importance of separating personal and professional dynamics. It was a challenging period, but Thomas's commitment to professional integrity gradually restored the team's morale and performance.

The Lesson

Thomas's story is a powerful reminder of the importance of professional boundaries in leadership. Personal relationships, when not managed carefully, can significantly impact team dynamics and decision-making. Leaders must be vigilant in maintaining a balance between being approachable and upholding the standards and objectivity required in their professional roles.

Building a Professional Team Culture:
A Tale of Two Leaders

CASE STUDY 1: THE SUCCESS OF LEADER A

In the heart of Silicon Valley, Leader A, named Sarah, took the helm of a tech startup. Sarah was known for her exceptional leadership skills and her ability to foster a culture of respect and productivity. She inherited a team that was diverse in skills and personalities. Among them were a few she had known from her previous job, sharing a friendly rapport.

Strategies for Success:

Clear Communication of Expectations: From day one, Sarah communicated her expectations clearly. She emphasized the importance of respect, accountability, and professionalism.

Establishing Boundaries: Despite having friends on the team, Sarah made it clear that professional decisions would be based solely on merit and business needs.

Inclusive Decision Making: She involved the team in decision-making processes, ensuring everyone felt heard and valued.

Regular Feedback: Sarah implemented a system of regular, constructive feedback that applied to everyone, including her friends.

Outcome:

The team thrived under Sarah's leadership. The clear boundaries and inclusive culture led to high morale, innovation, and impressive productivity. Her friends respected her professional approach, understanding the separation between work and personal life.

- How clearly do you communicate your expectations to your team?

- Are you consistent in applying rules and feedback to all team members?

CASE STUDY 2: THE DOWNFALL OF LEADER B

Conversely, in a financial firm in New York, Leader B, named Jack, faced a different scenario. Jack was promoted to a managerial position and was excited to lead a team that included several of his close friends.

Strategies That Led to Failure:

Lack of Clear Boundaries: Jack often blurred the lines between friendship and leadership. He avoided giving constructive feedback to his friends, fearing it might hurt their feelings.

Favoritism: His friends received preferential treatment, often excused from tight deadlines and critical tasks.

Informal Decision Making: Many decisions were made during casual, after-work gatherings, excluding non-friend team members.

Outcome:

The team's performance began to suffer. Non-friend team members felt demotivated and overlooked, leading to a toxic work environment. The lack of clear leadership and favoritism eroded the team's respect for Jack, culminating in poor overall performance and high turnover.

- Do you find it challenging to provide honest feedback to friends in your team?

- Are you aware of any favoritism in your decision-making?

Conclusion

These contrasting case studies of Sarah and Jack highlight the critical importance of establishing and maintaining professional boundaries in leadership. While Sarah's approach led to a high-performing team, Jack's inability to separate personal relationships from professional responsibilities resulted in team dysfunction. As a leader, assessing your current team dynamics with these reflective questions can guide you in fostering a culture that balances respect, productivity, and professional integrity.

As we close this chapter on the intricate dance of leadership and professional boundaries, it's clear that the journey of learning and growth is ongoing. To further enrich your understanding and provide additional perspectives on this crucial aspect of leadership, I highly recommend exploring some key resources that delve deeper into these themes.

Firstly, "Leaders Eat Last: Why Some Teams Pull Together and Others Don't" by Simon Sinek is an essential read. Sinek masterfully explores the concept of leadership as a duty to others rather than a position of power. He provides insightful guidance on how leaders can cultivate trust and cooperation within their teams, which is fundamental in achieving success and high performance. This book is particularly enlightening in understanding how to balance being a supportive leader while maintaining those all-important professional boundaries. Find "Leaders Eat Last" on Amazon.

Next, "The Five Dysfunctions of a Team: A Leadership Fable" by Patrick Lencioni offers a compelling model for building a unified and effective team. Lencioni identifies key challenges teams often face, such as a lack of trust and avoidance of conflict, issues that become more pronounced in the absence of clear professional boundaries. This narrative is an invaluable resource for comprehending the nuances of team dynamics and the pivotal role of a leader in nurturing a positive team environment. Find "The Five Dysfunctions of a Team" on Amazon.

Lastly, for a broader spectrum of insights, the Harvard Business Review's articles on Leadership and Team Management are indispensable. Covering a range of topics from maintaining professional boundaries to effective communication and leadership strategies, these articles are penned by seasoned professionals and scholars. They offer a blend of theoretical and practical wisdom that can be applied in various leadership contexts. Explore HBR's Leadership and Managing People Topic.

Each of these resources will provide you with deeper insights and practical strategies to enhance your leadership journey. As you continue to navigate the complexities of leadership, remember that the learning never stops, and each step forward is an opportunity to grow and inspire.

CHAPTER 2

The Art of Thoughtful Change

"Leadership thrives on careful consideration, not haste;
understand the ground before planting the seeds of change."

Let's Talk Culture

Hey there, let's dive into something really crucial in leadership – understanding your organization's culture. Think of it like a sailor who knows the sea like the back of his hand. He's not just steering the ship; he's reading the waves, the wind, and the weather. That's what we're doing with organizational culture. We're not just making changes; we're feeling the pulse of the place, getting the vibe, and then moving forward. It's all about the journey, not just the destination.

Many leaders believe in making changes quickly due to a combination of factors. Often, they feel pressure to demonstrate their impact and validate their leadership, especially when newly appointed. There's a common perception that swift action signifies strength and decisiveness, qualities traditionally valued in leadership. Additionally, in today's fast-paced business environment, there's a prevailing sense that rapid adaptation is necessary to stay competitive and relevant. This mindset can lead to a belief that quick changes are essential for driving innovation and achieving immediate results, even though this approach may overlook the importance of thorough planning and stakeholder engagement.

A Tale of Two Leaders

Alex's story is a cautionary tale about the pitfalls of rushing into change without fully understanding the unique dynamics of a new environment. When Alex stepped into the CEO role at a cutting-edge tech company, he was brimming with confidence and ideas. He had a successful track record and was known for his dynamic leadership style. Eager to imprint his vision, Alex immediately set about implementing a series of sweeping changes.

In his first week, Alex introduced a new organizational structure, aiming to streamline operations. He dismantled several teams and merged others, believing this would foster efficiency. However, he didn't realize that these teams had evolved organically over years, developing systems and relationships that were crucial to their success. The restructuring disrupted these workflows, leading to confusion and frustration among employees.

Alex also decided to fast-track the development of a new software product, pushing the team to cut down the development cycle by half. This decision was made without consulting the product development team, who were already working at capacity on existing projects. The accelerated timeline put immense pressure on the team, leading to burnout and a decline in the quality of work.

Moreover, Alex introduced a new performance evaluation system, one he had used successfully in his previous company. This system was more aggressive and metrics-driven, a stark contrast to the more collaborative and developmental approach the company was used to. It created a competitive atmosphere that was alien to the company's culture of teamwork and mutual support.

The fallout from these changes was significant. Long-standing employees, who were the backbone of the company's culture and success, felt alienated and undervalued. Many of them, unable to adapt to the new way of working, chose to leave. This exodus of talent caused a ripple effect, impacting morale and productivity. New hires, brought in to replace them, struggled to fill the gaps due to the loss of institutional knowledge.

Customers also felt the impact. The rushed software product pushed hastily to market, was riddled with bugs and received poor reviews. This damaged the company's reputation for quality and innovation, leading to a loss of trust among its customer base.

Alex's failure to understand the existing culture and processes of the company, and his haste in implementing changes, led to a series of missteps. It was a tough lesson in the importance of taking the time to understand the unique ecosystem of an organization before attempting to transform it. His story serves as a reminder that leadership is as much about listening and learning as it is about directing and deciding.

Slow and Steady Wins the Race

Maria's journey to effective change in her healthcare organization is a testament to the power of patience and understanding in leadership. When she first stepped into her role, she resisted the urge to immediately implement her vision. Instead, Maria chose a path of observation and engagement, a decision that would profoundly shape her approach to change.

In her first few weeks, Maria embarked on a 'listening tour' across the organization. She held meetings with teams from various departments, not to dictate but to ask questions and genuinely listen. She walked the halls, engaged with staff at all levels, and even spent time understanding the day-to-day challenges faced by frontline workers. Maria knew that to lead effectively, she first needed to understand the heart of the organization – its people.

As she absorbed the culture, Maria began to notice patterns and areas that needed improvement. However, she didn't rush to make changes. Instead, she started small, focusing on areas where quick wins could build trust and demonstrate her commitment to the team's well-being. For instance, she first tackled the long-standing issue of inefficient scheduling that staff had complained about. By introducing a more flexible system, she immediately improved the work-life balance for many employees, winning their trust and goodwill.

Maria's approach to larger changes was equally methodical. Before revamping the patient care model – a significant shift for the organization – she spent months preparing the ground. She formed a diverse change committee, including representatives from every level of staff, to ensure a wide range of perspectives. Together, they co-created a plan, which Maria communicated transparently to the entire organization, explaining the rationale and expected benefits.

Even as changes were implemented, Maria remained open to feedback. She held regular town hall meetings where employees could voice their concerns and suggestions. This open dialogue helped to refine the changes continuously, making them more effective and less disruptive.

The impact of Maria's slow and steady approach was profound. Not only were the changes more successful, but they were also sustainable. Employees felt heard and valued, leading to higher engagement and morale. The organization began to operate more efficiently, patient satisfaction scores improved, and the staff turnover rate decreased.

Maria's story is a powerful example of how taking the time to understand an organization's culture, engaging with stakeholders at all levels, and implementing changes gradually can lead to successful and lasting trans-formation. Her leadership style highlights that sometimes, being slow to make changes is the quickest path to achieving long-term success.

When Rushing Backfires

But it's not always a success story. Take this big retail company that decided to flip its inventory system overnight. They didn't really check in with the folks on the ground, and boy, did it backfire. Stock was all over the place, employees were stressed, and customers weren't happy. They had to back-track and it cost them big time. It's a classic example of why rushing into things without getting everyone's input can really mess things up.

Tips for Making Change Work

So, how do you make change work? First, really get to know your organi-zation – its culture, values, and how things are done. Then, when you're ready to make changes, talk about it. Get everyone involved and listen to what they have to say. Keep an eye on how things are going and be ready to tweak your plans. And don't forget to celebrate the small victories along the way – they really add up!

Some Food for Thought

Think about how well you really know your organization. Are you involv-ing everyone in your plans for change? How do you balance shaking things up with keeping things stable?

Wrapping It Up

Remember, leading change is more about the journey than just hitting a target. It's about patience, really understanding where you are, and mov-ing forward with everyone's input. By taking a thoughtful, people-focused approach, you can guide your organization to new heights, avoiding the pitfalls of rushing in without a map. Let's make change a positive, inclusive journey, shall we?

As we wrap up our exploration of the nuanced art of implementing change in leadership, it's clear that this journey is rich with learning opportunities. For those eager to dive deeper and expand their understanding, I highly recommend these three insightful books. Each offers a unique perspective on change management, from the strategic steps in "Leading Change" to the psychological insights in "Switch," and the powerful, people-centered approach in "The Heart of Change." These readings will not only complement the lessons from this chapter but also enrich your overall approach to leading transformative change in your organization. Happy reading, and may your journey through change be as enlightening as it is impactful!

CHAPTER 3

Harvesting Low-Hanging Fruits

"Capitalize on the readily available victories to build momentum;
every small win is a step towards monumental success."

The Misconception of the Herculean Test
"Many people believe that to truly prove their worth, they must tackle the most formidable challenges head-on. This belief often leads to overlooking simpler, yet equally impactful opportunities. It's like a climber who, intent on conquering the highest peak, fails to notice the beautiful, accessible paths that also lead to breathtaking views. This chapter challenges the notion that complexity and difficulty are the only measures of success. Instead, it invites you to explore the power of low-hanging fruits – those opportunities that are easily within our reach but often ignored in the pursuit of more daunting tasks.

Imagine a world where leaders, instead of constantly seeking the most challenging test to prove a point, turn their attention to the simpler, achievable tasks that can yield significant results. This approach is not about taking the easy way out; it's about being smart and strategic in how we choose our battles. It's about understanding that sometimes, the most straightforward solutions can lead to the most profound impacts.

In this chapter, we will delve into stories and case studies that illuminate the value of seizing these accessible opportunities. We will explore how focusing on easy wins can build momentum, establish credibility, and set a positive tone for your leadership journey. From the tale of a manager who transformed her team's morale with a simple change, to the story of a CEO who missed out on significant opportunities by overlooking the obvious, these narratives will provide you with a new perspective on the power of low-hanging fruits.

So, let's embark on this journey together, rethinking our approach to challenges and leadership. Let's discover how, by focusing on the attainable and the manageable, we can achieve remarkable success and inspire those around us to do the same. Welcome to a chapter that promises not just insights but a transformation in the way you perceive and approach your leadership challenges."

Seizing the Easy Wins

In the journey of leadership, the art of identifying and capitalizing on easy wins – or 'low-hanging fruits' – is invaluable. These are opportunities that require minimal effort but yield significant results. They are not just about quick fixes; they're strategic moves that can set a positive tone, build momentum, and establish credibility. For a leader, these early successes are crucial in gaining the trust and confidence of their team, demonstrating their capability, and laying a foundation for more substantial changes.

ANECDOTE: SARAH'S SWIFT SOLUTION

When Sarah joined the marketing firm as a manager, she walked into an environment brimming with talent but bogged down by low morale. The team, once vibrant and productive, was now struggling under the weight of cumbersome weekly reporting processes. Reports that should have taken minutes stretched into hours, eating into the time that could have been spent on creative endeavors.

Sarah, with her keen eye for efficiency, quickly identified this as a low-hanging fruit – a problem that was simple yet impactful. She set to work, consulting with her team to understand the specific pain points of the existing system. Together, they brainstormed and implemented a streamlined reporting process, one that utilized automation tools and eliminated redundant steps.

The change was small in scope but monumental in its effect. The team's morale soared as they reclaimed hours of lost productivity. They were now able to focus on what they did best – being creative. Sarah's quick action not only boosted the team's efficiency but also earned her their respect and trust. It set a positive tone for her leadership, proving that sometimes the most significant victories come from solving the simplest problems.

CASE STUDY 1: TOM'S WELLNESS WEDNESDAYS

Tom, a school principal, faced a different challenge. He noticed a worrying trend of teacher burnout in his school. Teachers, the backbone of the educational system, were overwhelmed with administrative tasks and continuous professional development requirements, leaving them little time for self-care or relaxation.

Understanding the importance of teacher well-being, Tom introduced 'Wellness Wednesdays.' On these days, one hour of professional development was replaced with activities focused on relaxation and mental health – yoga sessions, mindfulness workshops, or even just a quiet hour for reading or personal reflection.

This initiative, though small in scale, had a ripple effect throughout the school. Teachers felt more valued and cared for, leading to a noticeable improvement in their morale. This, in turn, reflected in their teaching, with students benefiting from more engaged and energized educators. Absenteeism among teachers decreased, and the overall atmosphere in the school became more positive and supportive. Tom's 'Wellness Wednesdays' demonstrated how addressing a simple need could lead to significant improvements in the overall health of an organization.

CASE STUDY 2: THE TECH STARTUP'S OVERSIGHT

In contrast, the story of a tech startup serves as a cautionary tale. The CEO, a visionary obsessed with cutting-edge innovations, failed to notice the cracks forming in the foundation of his company. Basic operational inefficiencies, such as poor communication channels and a convoluted project management process, were hindering progress and frustrating employees.

Despite feedback from team members, these simple yet critical issues were consistently overlooked in favor of more glamorous, innovative projects. The result was a gradual erosion of employee satisfaction and efficiency. Talented staff members, feeling unheard and undervalued, began to leave. The company, once a beacon of innovation, found itself struggling to maintain its edge due to high turnover and operational chaos.

This scenario underscores the importance of addressing basic operational needs and listening to employee feedback. It shows that innovation, while vital, should not come at the cost of fundamental organizational health. The CEO's failure to capitalize on easy wins – improving communication and streamlining processes – ultimately cost the company its most valuable asset: its people.

PRACTICAL TIPS: FINDING AND LEVERAGING EASY WINS

Listen and Observe: Spend time understanding your team's daily challenges. Often, easy wins can be found in addressing everyday frustrations.

Prioritize Impact: Focus on changes that offer the most significant impact with the least complexity.

Communicate and Involve: Share your plans for these changes and involve your team in the implementation process.

Celebrate Successes: Recognize and celebrate these early wins to boost morale and build confidence in your leadership.

REFLECTIVE QUESTIONS

Are you actively looking for easy wins within your team or organization?

How can you better listen to and observe your team to identify these opportunities?

In what ways can you ensure that these wins are stepping stones to larger goals?

In summary, harvesting low-hanging fruits is about more than just quick wins; it's a strategic approach to building a strong foundation for future success. By identifying and capitalizing on these opportunities, you can set a positive tone, build confidence among your team members, and pave the way for more significant achievements. Remember, the journey of a thousand miles begins with a single step – or in the case of effective leadership, with the first easy win.

As we conclude our exploration of the strategic value of low-hanging fruits in leadership, it's clear that this approach is both an art and a science. For those eager to delve deeper into this topic, the above books provide a wealth of knowledge and practical strategies. From the critical first steps in "The First 90 Days" to the transformative insights in "Good to Great," and the profound concept of "Small Wins," these readings will not only complement the lessons from this chapter but also enrich your overall approach to leadership. They offer a deeper understanding of how small, strategic actions can lead to significant, lasting change. So, as you continue on your leadership journey, let these resources guide and inspire you to find and leverage those easy wins that can propel you and your organization to greater heights. Happy reading, and may your path be marked by many fruitful victories!

CHAPTER 4

Navigating Pre-Existing Relationships as a New Leader

"Leading with professionalism, irrespective of personal ties, ensures fairness and integrity in every decision."

Introduction: Entering the Labyrinth of Legacy Bonds

Imagine stepping into a leadership role as akin to entering a labyrinth. The paths are the complex web of pre-existing relationships within your new organization. These relationships, invisible to the untrained eye, are the threads that weave the fabric of the team's culture. They influence everything from daily interactions to strategic decisions. As a new leader, your challenge is not just to navigate this maze but to understand and harmonize these legacy bonds for the betterment of your team and organization.

The Unseen Ties and Their Silent Power

Picture yourself as a new leader walking into a room where every glance, every nod, carries a history you're not privy to. This is the reality of stepping into an established team. Here, alliances have been formed, rivalries have simmered, and unspoken agreements dictate the uncharted territories of team dynamics. Your success hinges on your ability to discern these invisible ties and manage them with tact and insight.

CASE STUDY 1: LISA'S DIPLOMATIC MASTERY

Lisa's story begins when she assumed the role of head of a marketing department. She walked into a team where creativity met chaos. Two team members, both talented but at odds, had created an undercurrent of tension affecting the entire department. Lisa, with her astute observational skills, quickly picked up on the silent exchanges and the unspoken discomfort among the team.

Determined to address this, Lisa embarked on a journey of diplomatic navigation. She initiated one-on-one conversations with each of the feuding parties, not to judge or take sides, but to understand. She listened, empathized, and then carefully orchestrated a mediated session where both parties could air their grievances in a controlled environment. This intervention was not just about resolving a feud; it was about setting a new standard of communication and conflict resolution.

The result was transformative. The feud was not only resolved, but the process also fostered a culture of openness and respect. Lisa's approach demonstrated that understanding and addressing underlying tensions can lead to a more cohesive and productive team environment.

CASE STUDY 2: MARK'S OVERSIGHT AND ITS REPERCUSSIONS

Mark's journey as a new sales team leader was less fortuitous. He entered a team where camaraderie masked underlying complexities. Two of his direct reports, who were close friends, presented a unique challenge – a fact Mark was oblivious to. His decisions, though well-intentioned, began to inadvertently favor one over the other. This bias, though unintended, did not go unnoticed.

The impact was immediate and profound. The team, once united, started to fracture. Rumors of favoritism spread, trust in Mark's leadership waned, and the team's performance suffered. Mark's failure to recognize and address the dynamics of pre-existing relationships led to a divided team and a toxic work environment.

His story serves as a cautionary tale about the importance of being aware of and sensitive to the existing relationships within a team. It highlights the need for new leaders to observe, understand, and thoughtfully navigate the intricate web of interpersonal dynamics they inherit.

In conclusion, both Lisa and Mark's stories underscore the critical role that understanding and managing pre-existing relationships play in effective leadership. While Lisa's story exemplifies the power of insightful and pro-active management, Mark's experience serves as a reminder of the pitfalls of neglecting the undercurrents of team dynamics. As a leader, your ability to discern and harmoniously navigate these pre-existing relationships is key to fostering a positive, productive, and unified team.

PRACTICAL TIPS: NAVIGATING PRE-EXISTING RELATIONSHIPS

Observe and Inquire: Spend time observing team interactions and ask open-ended questions to understand the team's dynamics.

Maintain Neutrality: Avoid taking sides in existing conflicts. Approach each situation with an unbiased perspective.

Foster Open Communication: Create an environment where team members feel comfortable discussing their concerns and relationships.

Seek Mentorship: Consult with a mentor or a more experienced leader who can provide insights into handling such situations.

How can you better identify pre-existing relationships within your team?

What strategies can you employ to ensure you remain impartial and fair in your leadership?

How can you foster a culture of transparency and open communication to address hidden tensions?

In conclusion, as a new leader, understanding and adeptly managing pre-existing relationships within your team is vital. It requires keen observation, open communication, and a fair, unbiased approach. By doing so, you can navigate these invisible ties, foster a positive team environment, and lead more effectively.

As we wrap up our exploration of navigating the intricate web of pre-existing relationships in leadership, it's clear that this is a nuanced and vital skill for any leader stepping into a new role. The above books are invaluable resources for those looking to delve deeper into this subject. From the strategic insights in "The First 90 Days" to the profound lessons in "Leadership and Self-Deception," and the practical tools offered in "Crucial Conversations," these readings will not only complement the insights from this chapter but also enhance your overall leadership toolkit. They provide a deeper understanding of how to effectively manage and navigate the complex interpersonal dynamics that are part and parcel of any leadership role. So, as you continue to develop your leadership skills, let these resources be your guide in mastering the art of understanding and harmonizing pre-existing relationships within your team. Happy reading, and may your leadership journey be enriched with strong, positive, and productive relationships!

CHAPTER 5

The Unspoken Realities of Leadership

"Leadership carries the weight of unspoken challenges; the strength to bear them silently is what truly defines a leader."

Welcome to Chapter 5, where we pull back the curtain on the less glamorous, often brutal truths of leadership. This chapter is a reality check, a necessary grounding for any aspiring or new leader. Here, we confront the unspoken challenges that come with the mantle of leadership – challenges that are seldom discussed in conventional leadership narratives but are crucial for anyone stepping into this role.

The Brutal Truth: Leadership is Not a Hero's Journey, It's a Balancing Act

The brutal truth is this: leadership is not always about being the hero at the forefront of every battle. It's not just about vision and inspiration. It's a complex balancing act that involves managing your own emotions while navigating the intricate web of organizational politics. It's about making tough decisions that won't always be popular. It's about facing the loneliness that often accompanies the responsibility of being at the top.

As a new leader, you will be tested – not just in your professional skills but in your emotional resilience, your ethical compass, and your ability to maintain your humanity in the face of relentless pressure. This chapter is your guide through these uncharted waters, offering insights and strategies to help you emerge as a leader who is not only successful but also grounded, empathetic, and true to your values.

Welcome to the real world of leadership. It's challenging, it's demanding, but it's also incredibly rewarding for those who are prepared to embrace its complexities.

Leadership is often romanticized as a journey of inspiring speeches and grand visions. However, beneath this glossy surface lies a complex world of emotional labor, political navigation, and relentless decision-making. This chapter delves into these less-discussed but equally critical aspects of leadership, offering a more holistic view of what it truly means to lead.

The Weight of Emotional Labor

Consider the story of Emily, a seasoned executive in a multinational corporation. Her journey wasn't just about strategic decisions and market expansions; it was equally about managing emotions – her own and her team's. Emily's ability to empathize with her team, absorb their stress during tough times, and remain a pillar of strength was as crucial to her success as her business acumen.

CASE STUDY 1: NAVIGATING THE POLITICAL LANDSCAPE

In a positive scenario, let's explore the story of Raj, a department head in a large tech firm. Raj understood that organizational politics were not just about power plays; they were about building relationships, understanding various interests, and navigating them to achieve goals. He used his political savvy to advocate for his team, secure resources, and influence key decisions, all while maintaining his integrity and fostering a positive work environment.

CASE STUDY 2: THE COST OF IGNORING ORGANIZATIONAL POLITICS

On the flip side, there's the story of Anna, a talented leader who chose to stay away from any form of office politics. Her reluctance to engage in the organizational dynamics led to her team being overlooked for important projects, missing out on critical resources, and ultimately feeling undervalued. Anna's story highlights the importance of engaging with, rather than avoiding, the political aspects of leadership.

PRACTICAL TIPS: EMBRACING THE FULL SPECTRUM OF LEADERSHIP

Emotional Intelligence: Cultivate the ability to understand and manage your emotions and those of others.

Political Acumen: Learn to navigate organizational politics positively and ethically.

Decision-Making Stamina: Develop resilience in facing constant decision-making pressures.

Self-Care: Prioritize your well-being to sustain your effectiveness as a leader.

REFLECTIVE QUESTIONS

How do you manage the emotional labor that comes with leadership?

In what ways can you engage more effectively in organizational politics?

How do you maintain your decision-making effectiveness over prolonged periods?

What self-care practices do you have in place to support your leadership journey?

In conclusion, leadership is more than just guiding a team towards a common goal. It's about managing the unspoken, often challenging aspects of the role – the emotional labor, the political navigation, and the relentless decision-making. By acknowledging and skillfully managing these realities, you can become a more effective, resilient, and empathetic leader, capable of guiding your team through the complexities of the modern workplace.

As we move forward from the raw and honest revelations of this Chapter, it's important to continue our journey of growth and understanding. The books recommended are not just readings; they are tools for deeper insight and practical application. From enhancing your emotional intelligence with Goleman's expertise to navigating the perils of leadership with Heifetz and Linsky, and understanding the transformational qualities of great leaders with Collins, these resources will guide you through the complexities of leadership. They offer a blend of theoretical knowledge and practical wisdom, essential for anyone aspiring to lead with integrity, resilience, and empathy. So, as you step into the challenging yet rewarding world of leadership, let these books be your companions, illuminating the path towards becoming a leader who not only achieves success but also inspires and uplifts those around them.

CHAPTER 6

Trust but Verify: A Balanced Approach

"In leadership, trust lays the foundation, but verification builds the structure; together, they create an unshakeable edifice of accountability."

A Turn of Tables: From Mentee to Mentor in Nursing

As we step into Chapter 6, let me share a personal story that perfectly encapsulates the essence of this chapter's theme: the critical balance between trust and verification in leadership.

Several years ago, as a fresh-faced nurse, I started my journey on a telemetry floor. There, I was precepted by Jenna, an experienced and highly skilled nurse. Jenna's guidance was invaluable; she was a mentor who instilled in me the fundamentals of nursing care and the nuances of patient management in a high-paced environment.

Fast forward a few years, I transitioned to the Intensive Care Unit (ICU), a realm that demanded a higher level of clinical acumen and decision-making skills. As I grew in my role, I eventually became a preceptor myself, guiding new nurses as they navigated the complexities of critical care.

In an interesting twist of fate, Jenna, my original preceptor from the telemetry floor, joined the ICU team. The dynamic of our relationship shifted; I was now the mentor, and she was the mentee in this new setting. It was a role reversal that brought with it a unique set of challenges and learning opportunities.

One day, I assigned Jenna a critical task, confident in her abilities and the trust we had built over the years. However, in my confidence, I overlooked a crucial aspect of leadership – verification. I failed to verify that the task was completed correctly. This oversight led to a significant learning moment for both of us. It highlighted the importance of maintaining a balance between trusting your team and ensuring that tasks are completed accurately, especially in a high-stakes environment like the ICU.

This experience serves as a powerful introduction to the core message of this chapter: In leadership, trust is fundamental, but verification is essential. It's a delicate dance, especially in fields where the stakes are high and the margin for error is slim. As we delve deeper into this chapter, we will explore strategies and insights on how to master this balance, ensuring both the empowerment of your team and the excellence in performance that your leadership role demands.

Introduction: Unraveling the Paradox of Trust

In the intricate dance of leadership, the paradox of trust plays a central role. It's about nurturing a culture of trust while simultaneously upholding a framework of accountability. This chapter delves into the nuanced journey of leaders like Clara, a project manager in a tech company, who exemplified this balance. Clara's leadership was characterized by her commitment to building a foundation of trust with her team. She encouraged open dialogue, fostered a sense of empowerment among her team members, and championed a culture of mutual respect. However, Clara was equally vigilant in implementing systematic progress checks and establishing clear accountability measures. This dual approach did not just cultivate a trusting environment; it also guaranteed high performance and adherence to organizational standards.

CASE STUDY 1: THE SYMPHONY OF TRUST AND VERIFICATION

James's story, a school principal, serves as a beacon of positive leadership. James understood the delicate equilibrium between trust and verification. He placed immense trust in his teachers, respecting their expertise and granting them the autonomy they needed in their classrooms. Yet, he didn't stop there. James also instituted a robust system of regular feedback and performance reviews. This strategy wasn't about micromanagement; it was about maintaining a pulse on the school's health. The result was a thriving educational environment where trust and high morale were the norm, leading to outstanding academic achievements.

CASE STUDY 2: THE PITFALLS OF OVERRELIANCE ON TRUST

In stark contrast stands Lisa's tale, a startup founder whose leadership journey was marred by an overreliance on trust. Lisa's philosophy was simple: trust above everything else. However, this approach led her down a perilous path. The absence of verification mechanisms and oversight in her startup resulted in a cascade of negative outcomes - missed deadlines, inconsistent work quality, and the eventual failure of critical projects. Lisa's story is a cautionary tale about the dangers of blind trust in the absence of verification.

PRACTICAL TIPS: CRAFTING THE PERFECT BALANCE

Setting Clear Expectations: It begins with clarity. Clearly articulate your expectations and the performance standards you seek.

Regular Check-Ins: Implement a system of regular progress reviews. This isn't about breathing down people's necks; it's about staying informed and involved.

Empower but Verify: Empower your team with autonomy but pair it with a mechanism to verify outcomes. It's about trust, with a safety net.

Cultivating a Feedback Culture: Create an environment where feedback flows freely and regularly. It's a two-way street that fosters growth and improvement.

REFLECTIVE QUESTIONS

How do you currently balance trust and verification in your leadership approach?

What systems or processes do you have in place to ensure accountability while fostering trust?

How do you navigate situations where trust has been compromised?

In what ways can you enhance the balance between empowering your team and maintaining effective oversight?

In conclusion, the essence of leadership lies in mastering the delicate balance between trust and verification. It's about creating an ecosystem where team members feel valued and trusted, yet there's a clear structure in place to ensure performance and standards are met. Achieving this balance is pivotal in building teams that are not just high-performing but also deeply committed and aligned with the broader vision of the organization.

In this Chapter, focusing on the intricate balance of trust and verification in leadership, I recommend three enriching resources. Stephen M.R.

Covey's "The Speed of Trust" explores the profound impact of trust in all aspects of life, particularly in leadership and organizational effectiveness. Daniel H. Pink's "Drive" delves into the true motivators behind human behavior, emphasizing the importance of autonomy, mastery, and purpose over external incentives, relevant for leaders managing empowerment and accountability. Additionally, the Harvard Business Review offers a comprehensive collection of articles on trust and accountability in leadership, providing research-based insights and practical strategies. These resources are invaluable for leaders seeking to deepen their understanding and enhance their ability to effectively balance trust with accountability in various organizational settings.

CHAPTER 7

Beyond the Throne: Navigating Hidden Leadership Dynamics

"True power in leadership lies not in dominance, but in the ability to inspire and uplift, guiding from the sidelines as much as from the front."

A Lesson in Unseen Influence: The Fall of a Promising Leader

Let me share a poignant story that underscores the essence of this chapter - a tale of an honest mistake with far-reaching consequences, highlighting the critical lesson that the most influential figures in an organization are not always the ones seated at the head of the table.

Meet Emily, a bright and ambitious professional who was recently promoted to a managerial position in a healthcare facility. Full of enthusiasm and fresh ideas, Emily was eager to make a positive impact. She was well aware of the formal hierarchy and focused her efforts on building strong relationships with the senior management team, confident that their support was key to implementing her vision.

However, Emily overlooked a crucial aspect of her new role - the informal power dynamics that existed within her team. There was Grace, a veteran nurse with decades of experience, who, despite not holding a formal leadership position, was highly respected and influential among her peers. Her opinions and perspectives often shaped the team's attitudes and decisions, a fact Emily was unaware of.

In her zeal to bring about change, Emily inadvertently sidelined Grace, failing to recognize her as a key stakeholder. This oversight led to resistance and skepticism from the team, who valued Grace's input and saw her exclusion as a sign of disrespect. Emily's initiatives, though well-intentioned, were met with lukewarm responses, and her credibility suffered.

It wasn't a glaring error or a deliberate act of negligence that led to Emily's downfall. It was a simple, honest mistake - a failure to understand the subtleties of hidden leadership dynamics within her team. This story serves as a powerful introduction to the complexities of leadership beyond the formal hierarchy. It's a reminder that success as a leader often hinges on recognizing and navigating the influence of those who, while not in official leadership roles, hold significant sway over the team's morale and decision-making.

ANECDOTE: THE UNSEEN CONDUCTOR - ALAN AND JENNA'S STORY

Alan, a new manager at a tech firm, faced the challenge of leading a team that was demoralized and resistant to change. He observed that Jenna, a senior developer, played a crucial but unofficial role in team dynamics. Jenna was not a manager, but her colleagues often turned to her for advice and support. She had a knack for explaining complex technical issues in a way that everyone could understand and was always the first to offer help when someone was struggling with a project.

Alan realized that Jenna's influence was a key to driving change. He started involving her in planning meetings, asking for her input on proposed changes. When he introduced a new project management tool, he first discussed it with Jenna, who provided valuable feedback on how it would be received by the team. She even helped tailor the training sessions for the team, making the transition smoother.

By acknowledging Jenna's role and making her an ally, Alan was able to implement changes with much less resistance. The team's morale improved, and productivity increased. Jenna's involvement in decision-making also helped her feel more valued and invested in the team's success.

CASE STUDY 1: HARNESSING THE POWER OF INFORMAL LEADERSHIP - RACHEL AND KEVIN'S JOURNEY

Rachel took over a marketing department that was struggling with low morale and high turnover. She noticed that Kevin, a graphic designer who had been with the company for over a decade, had a significant but unofficial influence over his colleagues. He was not a manager, but his opinion was highly valued, and he often served as a mentor to newer employees.

Rachel decided to leverage Kevin's influence to turn the department around. She began by having regular one-on-one meetings with him to understand the team's challenges from his perspective. She then involved him in developing a new strategy for the department, which included more collaborative projects and opportunities for professional development, areas Kevin was passionate about.

As Kevin became more involved in shaping the department's direction, the rest of the team became more engaged and enthusiastic. His endorsement of the new strategy helped to overcome skepticism and resistance from other team members. Under Rachel's leadership, with Kevin's support, the department's performance improved dramatically, with increased creativity and a significant reduction in staff turnover.

CASE STUDY 2: THE COST OF IGNORING UNSEEN INFLUENCERS - DAVID AND SARAH'S MISSTEP

David, a new sales team leader, was focused on establishing his authority and implementing his vision. He overlooked the informal networks within his team, particularly the influence of Sarah, a seasoned salesperson. Sarah was a mentor to many on the team and had a deep understanding of the company's clients and sales strategies.

David's failure to recognize and engage with Sarah led to several missteps. He introduced new sales targets and strategies without consulting the team, causing confusion and frustration. Sarah, feeling undervalued and ignored, became less engaged. Her change in attitude had a ripple effect on the team, leading to lower morale and decreased performance.

The team's sales numbers began to decline, and David faced increasing resistance to his initiatives. It was only after a significant drop in team performance that David realized the importance of Sarah's influence. By then, however, the damage to team cohesion and trust in his leadership had been done, illustrating the cost of ignoring the power of informal leaders within a team.

ANECDOTE: THE UNSEEN CONDUCTOR - ALAN AND JENNA'S STORY

Alan, a new manager at a tech firm, faced the challenge of leading a team that was demoralized and resistant to change. He observed that Jenna, a senior developer, played a crucial but unofficial role in team dynamics. Jenna was not a manager, but her colleagues often turned to her for advice and support. She had a knack for explaining complex technical issues in a way that everyone could understand and was always the first to offer help when someone was struggling with a project.

Alan realized that Jenna's influence was a key to driving change. He started involving her in planning meetings, asking for her input on proposed changes. When he introduced a new project management tool, he first discussed it with Jenna, who provided valuable feedback on how it would be received by the team. She even helped tailor the training sessions for the team, making the transition smoother.

By acknowledging Jenna's role and making her an ally, Alan was able to implement changes with much less resistance. The team's morale improved, and productivity increased. Jenna's involvement in decision-making also helped her feel more valued and invested in the team's success.

CASE STUDY 1: HARNESSING THE POWER OF INFORMAL LEADERSHIP - RACHEL AND KEVIN'S JOURNEY

Rachel took over a marketing department that was struggling with low morale and high turnover. She noticed that Kevin, a graphic designer who had been with the company for over a decade, had a significant but unofficial influence over his colleagues. He was not a manager, but his opinion was highly valued, and he often served as a mentor to newer employees.

Rachel decided to leverage Kevin's influence to turn the department around. She began by having regular one-on-one meetings with him to understand the team's challenges from his perspective. She then involved him in developing a new strategy for the department, which included more collaborative projects and opportunities for professional development, areas Kevin was passionate about.

As Kevin became more involved in shaping the department's direction, the rest of the team became more engaged and enthusiastic. His endorsement of the new strategy helped to overcome skepticism and resistance from other team members. Under Rachel's leadership, with Kevin's support, the department's performance improved dramatically, with increased creativity and a significant reduction in staff turnover.

CASE STUDY 2: THE COST OF IGNORING UNSEEN INFLUENCERS - DAVID AND SARAH'S MISSTEP

David, a new sales team leader, was focused on establishing his authority and implementing his vision. He overlooked the informal networks within his team, particularly the influence of Sarah, a seasoned salesperson. Sarah was a mentor to many on the team and had a deep understanding of the company's clients and sales strategies.

David's failure to recognize and engage with Sarah led to several missteps. He introduced new sales targets and strategies without consulting the team, causing confusion and frustration. Sarah, feeling undervalued and ignored, became less engaged. Her change in attitude had a ripple effect on the team, leading to lower morale and decreased performance.

The team's sales numbers began to decline, and David faced increasing resistance to his initiatives. It was only after a significant drop in team performance that David realized the importance of Sarah's influence. By then, however, the damage to team cohesion and trust in his leadership had been done, illustrating the cost of ignoring the power of informal leaders within a team.

PRACTICAL TIPS: NAVIGATING THE UNSEEN HIERARCHY

Observation is Key: Spend time observing team interactions to identify informal leaders.

Engage and Involve: Actively involve these influencers in decision-making processes.

Respect and Acknowledge: Show respect for their experience and insights.

Foster Open Communication: Encourage a culture where everyone feels heard, including unofficial leaders.

Balance Formal and Informal Dynamics: Strive to maintain a balance between respecting the formal hierarchy and the informal power structures.

REFLECTIVE QUESTIONS

Have you identified the informal leaders within your team or organization?

How can you better engage with these key influencers to enhance team dynamics?

In what ways can you balance the formal and informal leadership structures in your decision-making?

Reflect on a situation where recognizing an informal leader could have changed the outcome. What would you do differently?

In conclusion, effective leadership transcends formal titles and positions. It involves recognizing and navigating the complex web of informal power dynamics that exist within every organization. By understanding and leveraging these hidden influences, leaders can foster a more cohesive, responsive, and effective team environment.

As we conclude this chapter on the nuanced and often unseen aspects of leadership, it's important to continue exploring and understanding these dynamics beyond our discussion. To aid in this journey, I recommend three insightful books that delve deeper into the themes we've explored.

"Invisible Influence: The Hidden Forces that Shape Behavior" by Jonah Berger. Berger's book is an intriguing exploration of the subtle, often unnoticed forces that influence our behavior and decisions. For leaders, this understanding is crucial to navigate the unseen currents within organizations effectively. It's a must-read for those looking to grasp the less obvious aspects of leadership. Find "Invisible Influence" on Amazon

"Quiet: The Power of Introverts in a World That Can't Stop Talking" by Susan Cain In 'Quiet', Susan Cain sheds light on the power and potential of introverts, who are frequently the unseen influencers in a workplace. This book is invaluable for leaders striving to understand and leverage the strengths of all team members, especially those not in formal leadership roles but who still hold significant sway. Find "Quiet" on Amazon

"Leading from the Second Chair: Serving Your Church, Fulfilling Your Role, and Realizing Your Dreams" by Mike Bonem and Roger Patterson This book offers essential insights for those leading from positions other than the top of the hierarchy. It's a guide to effective leadership from the 'second chair', recognizing the influence and power that can come from these roles. A valuable read for understanding the dynamics of leadership beyond the traditional first-chair perspective. Find "Leading from the Second Chair" on Amazon

Each of these books provides a unique perspective on the themes of unseen influence and leadership from different vantage points. They are excellent resources for deepening your understanding and enhancing your leadership skills in a complex and ever-evolving organizational landscape.

CHAPTER 8

Grounded Leadership: Staying Connected

"Stay rooted in the realities of your team; a leader who keeps their ear to the ground hears the footsteps of change approaching."

In the dynamic and often tumultuous journey of leadership, there lies a profound, yet frequently overlooked virtue: staying grounded. Amidst the whirlwind of success and the relentless pressures of decision-making, this concept emerges as the bedrock of authentic leadership. It represents a harmonious blend of humility, self-awareness, and an unwavering connection to one's core values. These elements collectively serve as a guiding beacon, navigating leaders through the complexities of both their personal and professional lives. Grounded leadership is not just a style; it's a philosophy that underpins effective and authentic leadership. It's about maintaining a sense of normalcy and authenticity, ensuring that success, power, or external pressures do not detach one from their true self and the values that matter. This chapter delves into the essence of grounded leadership, providing insights and practical strategies to help leaders stay connected, balanced, and true to their core values, thereby fostering a culture of respect, learning, and holistic success.

In this chapter, we explore the journey of Emily, a new leader whose experiences epitomize the essence of staying grounded and connected. Emily's story is a testament to the power of humility and a deep understanding of the day-to-day realities of her team and organization. It's a narrative that underscores the importance of not allowing one's position to create a disconnect from those they lead.

Emily's Leadership Journey

Emily was promoted to a managerial position in a healthcare organization after years of working as a dedicated nurse. Her promotion was a significant leap, placing her in charge of a team she was once a part of. This transition brought unique challenges and opportunities for Emily to demonstrate grounded leadership.

Humble Beginnings: Emily's journey began at the bedside, providing direct patient care. Her hands-on experience in the trenches gave her a profound understanding of the challenges and realities her team faced daily. This experience became the foundation of her leadership approach.

Staying Connected: Despite her new role, Emily made it a point to stay connected with her team's day-to-day activities. She regularly spent time on the floor, not just as a supervisor, but as a participant in the care process. This involvement helped her make informed decisions and kept her empathetic to her team's needs.

Empathy and Approachability: Emily's background as a nurse made her approachable and relatable. Her team felt comfortable sharing their concerns and ideas with her, knowing she understood their perspective. This open communication fostered a strong, cohesive team environment.

Leading by Example: Emily led by example, often stepping in to assist with patient care during busy periods. Her willingness to roll up her sleeves and work alongside her team not only earned their respect but also reinforced a culture of teamwork and mutual support.

Balancing Leadership and Humility: Emily's biggest challenge was balancing her leadership responsibilities with her desire to remain a hands-on team member. She learned to delegate effectively, trust her team's abilities, and step back when necessary, all while maintaining her approachability and empathy.

ANECDOTE: THE DOWNFALL OF A DISCONNECTED LEADER

Let's delve deeper into the story of Tom, a dynamic CEO whose rapid ascent to the top echelons of his company is a tale of caution for aspiring leaders. Tom's journey began on the front lines, where his hands-on approach and keen understanding of the day-to-day operations earned him widespread respect and rapid promotions. Known for his ability to connect with his team and his insightful decision-making, Tom was the epitome of a leader in touch with his roots.

However, as Tom ascended the corporate ladder, a noticeable shift occurred. The higher he climbed, the more he distanced himself from the operational realities of his team. Meetings with senior executives and strategic planning sessions began to fill his calendar, gradually replacing the time he once spent on the ground with his team. This shift was subtle at first, but over time, Tom's connection with the day-to-day realities of his team's work began to fray.

This detachment was not immediately apparent in the company's performance, but cracks soon began to show. Tom started making strategic decisions based on high-level reports and second-hand information, losing sight of the nuances and challenges his team faced on the ground. He implemented new policies and strategies that, while impressive on paper, were misaligned with the actual capabilities of his team and the evolving market conditions.

The consequences of Tom's detachment were profound. Projects began to falter, as the strategies he devised were either too ambitious or out of sync with the practical realities of execution. His team, once motivated by his hands-on leadership, started feeling overlooked and undervalued. Their insights and feedback, which could have steered projects in the right direction, were no longer sought or heard.

The culmination of these missteps was a significant loss of business. Key clients, who had been loyal due to the company's previously stellar performance and understanding of their needs, began to look elsewhere as the quality and relevance of the services declined. Additionally, team morale plummeted, leading to a high turnover rate. The once cohesive and dynamic team environment that Tom had fostered was now a shadow of its former self.

Tom's story is a stark reminder of the perils of losing touch with the ground realities of one's team. His initial success was rooted in his ability to connect with and understand his team's work and challenges. However, his failure to maintain this connection as he moved up the corporate hierarchy led to a series of ill-informed decisions, disengagement of his team, and ultimately, a significant setback for the company he led.

CASE STUDY 1 (POSITIVE)

Benefits of a Leader Staying Well-Sarah, a regional manager of a retail chain, exemplifies the benefits of staying connected. Despite her busy schedule, she made regular store visits, engaging directly with employees and customers. This hands-on approach provided her with valuable insights into operational challenges and customer preferences, leading to strategic decisions that boosted sales and employee satisfaction.

CASE STUDY 2 (NEGATIVE): DETACHMENT LEADING TO POOR DECISION-MAKING

In contrast, there's the case of Alex, a department head in a tech company. Alex preferred to manage from a distance, relying solely on reports and meetings for information. This detachment from the day-to-day operations led to a misalignment between his strategies and the team's actual capabilities and market needs. The result was a series of failed projects and a demoralized team.

PRACTICAL TIPS: TECHNIQUES FOR STAYING CONNECTED AND INFORMED

Regular Team Interactions: Schedule frequent informal meetings or casual check-ins with your team.

Participate in Frontline Work: Occasionally work alongside your team to understand their daily challenges.

Open Communication Channels: Encourage open and honest feedback from all levels of the organization.

Empathy and Active Listening: Show genuine interest in your team's opinions and concerns.

Stay Informed on Industry Trends: Regularly update yourself on industry developments to make informed decisions.

REFLECTIVE QUESTIONS: SELF-ASSESSMENT ON CONNECTION WITH TEAM AND ORGANIZATIONAL REALITIES

How often do I engage in direct communication with my team?

Do I understand the daily challenges my team faces?

How do I ensure that my decisions are informed by on-the-ground realities?

What steps can I take to improve my connection with my team?

How can I better align my leadership decisions with the actual needs and capabilities of my team?

Conclusion

The Personal Pillars of Groundedness

Self-Awareness: This is the cornerstone of staying grounded. It involves a deep understanding of one's strengths, weaknesses, and the emotions that influence decisions. It's a journey of introspection, ensuring that actions align with the true self, preventing leaders from losing themselves in the facade of their roles.

Humility: In the face of success, humility acts as an anchor. It's the recognition that no matter the heights one reaches, there's always room to learn from others. This humility cultivates mutual respect and continuous learning, both within oneself and among team members.

Staying True to Core Values: Core values act as a compass amidst challenges and temptations. They guide decisions and actions, ensuring adherence to personal beliefs, irrespective of external pressures. This steadfastness garners respect and trust from those around.

Balance: Balance is crucial in staying grounded. It's about ensuring that success in one life aspect doesn't overshadow others. A grounded leader seeks harmony across work, personal life, and self-care, understanding that true success is multi-dimensional.

Connection to Roots: Remembering one's origins keeps a leader grounded. It involves maintaining connections with family, friends, and community, ensuring that success doesn't alter one's fundamental character. These connections remind leaders of their journey and the values that have shaped them.

Grounded Leadership in Action

Empathy and Approachability: Grounded leaders are relatable and empathetic, understanding and caring for their team members' well-being and development. This empathy fosters a supportive and open environment where everyone feels valued.

Realistic Expectations: Grounded leaders set achievable goals, understanding what their team can realistically accomplish. This approach avoids overambition, fostering a healthy, productive work environment.

Listening and Learning: Such leaders value all team members' opinions and ideas, promoting a culture of continuous learning and improvement. They recognize that great ideas can emerge from any level within the organization.

Visibility and Engagement: Staying connected with the day-to-day realities of the team is essential. It's about understanding their challenges and successes firsthand and being an active participant in the team's journey.

Leading by Example: Grounded leaders demonstrate the behaviors and values they expect from others. They lead from within the team, not from above, showing they are part of the journey, not just its guide.

Staying connected with your team's realities is a critical aspect of effective leadership. It involves a balanced approach of being a visionary while keeping your ear to the ground. By staying informed and empathetic to the experiences of your team, you can make decisions that are not only strategic but also supportive of the people you lead.

This chapter aims to guide leaders in understanding the importance of this connection and providing practical ways to maintain it.

As we conclude Chapter 8, which delves into the importance of staying grounded and connected in leadership, I'd like to recommend further readings that can deepen your understanding and provide additional perspectives on this vital topic. These resources will offer insights and strategies to help you maintain a grounded approach in your leadership journey.

"Mindful Leadership: The 9 Ways to Self-Awareness, Transforming Yourself, and Inspiring Others" by Maria Gonzalez

- Gonzalez's book is an excellent resource for leaders seeking to develop self-awareness and mindfulness. It provides practical guidance on how to stay grounded and connected with oneself and one's team.

"Leaders Eat Last: Why Some Teams Pull Together and Others Don't" by Simon Sinek

- Simon Sinek explores the importance of empathy and creating a culture of trust and support in leadership. This book is a great resource for understanding how to stay connected with your team and ensure their well-being.

"The Power of Humility: Choosing Peace over Conflict in Relationships" by Charles L. Whitfield

- While not exclusively about leadership, Whitfield's book delves into the power of humility in relationships. It offers insights into how humility can be a powerful tool for leaders to stay grounded and effectively connect with others.

As we move forward, these readings can serve as valuable companions, offering guidance and inspiration on your path to becoming a more grounded and connected leader. They provide practical advice and profound insights into maintaining humility, self-awareness, and a strong connection with your team and organizational realities.

CHAPTER 9

Balancing Realism and Idealism

"A leader's art is to balance dreams with reality, crafting
a vision that is as inspiring as it is achievable."

Imagine you're the captain of a spaceship, navigating through the vast, starry universe. This journey is a lot like leadership, a thrilling adventure where two guiding stars, Realism and Idealism, help you find your way.

Realism in Leadership: Think of realism as your spaceship's control panel, full of buttons and screens showing you exactly what's happening right now. Realistic leaders, like skilled pilots, use this information to make smart decisions. They know how much fuel they have (resources), how fast they can go (team capabilities), and what obstacles might be in their path (risks). They set courses that they know they can reach and solve problems by looking at what tools and options they have right at that moment.

Idealism in Leadership: Now, idealism is like the beautiful, distant planets and galaxies you dream of exploring. Idealistic leaders are like the dreamers on board, imagining incredible destinations. They inspire everyone with stories of these far-off places, full of hope and excitement. They plan for big, bold adventures and encourage everyone to think of new, creative ways to travel further and faster. They remind everyone why the journey is so important and keep their eyes on the stars, representing their highest hopes and values.

The Magic of Balancing Both: The best space captains know how to use both their control panel (realism) and their telescope (idealism). They inspire their crew with visions of new galaxies (big goals) while making sure they have enough fuel and a safe path to get there (practical planning). This balance makes the journey exciting but also safe and successful. They keep dreaming of new worlds but also enjoy and learn from the stars and planets they pass along the way.

So, as we dive into this chapter, think of yourself as a space captain. How will you balance the realistic details of piloting your ship with the exciting dreams of exploring new galaxies? Let's embark on this adventure together and discover how to be a leader who can dream big and also make those dreams come true

Let's step into the world of Emily, a leader with a heart full of dreams and a mind buzzing with ideas. Her journey begins in a cozy, somewhat chaotic office, surrounded by a small team of passionate individuals. Together, they shared a vision that seemed larger than life: to transform the way people interact with technology, making it not just a tool, but a natural extension of their lives. Emily's dream wasn't just a business plan; it was a promise of a brighter future, and her team believed in it wholeheartedly.

As they set out on this adventure, Emily faced a challenge that touches the soul of every leader: finding harmony between the soaring dreams that inspire us and the hard, often stubborn realities of the world. Emily's vision was like a lighthouse, guiding their journey, but the sea they navigated was unpredictable, filled with obstacles and limited resources that often seemed to conspire against them.

In those early days, Emily's boundless idealism sometimes found itself at odds with the practical needs of her team. She urged them forward, setting ambitious targets, driven by the belief that they could achieve the extraordinary. But reality has a way of bringing even the most soaring spirits back to earth. Deadlines slipped by, the team's energy began to fray, and the once bright dream started to dim under the weight of unmet expectations.

This was a defining moment for Emily. She stood at a crossroads, where she could either cling to her original vision with unyielding determination, risking the well-being and morale of her team, or she could pause, listen, and learn. With a heart open to change, Emily chose the latter. She gathered her team, not as a leader dictating terms, but as a fellow traveler seeking guidance. Together, they reshaped their goals into something more attainable, yet still infused with the spirit of their original dream.

This change marked a new beginning for the startup. The team, now working towards clear, realistic objectives, rediscovered their enthusiasm. Progress began to accelerate, not because their vision had shrunk, but because they had found a more sustainable path to chase it. Emily's leadership had transformed; she had learned the delicate art of balancing dreams with reality, of guiding her team with a vision that was both aspirational and attainable.

Emily's story is a heartfelt reminder for all leaders who dare to dream big. It shows us that while our idealism is the spark that ignites change and innovation, our realism is the anchor that keeps our journey steady and sustainable. In this chapter, we delve into the heart of this balance, offering insights and strategies for leaders to inspire their teams with dreams that reach for the stars, while keeping their feet firmly planted in the realities of what can be achieved.

ANECDOTE: THE TIGHTROPE OF DREAMS AND REALITY

Meet Alex, a young entrepreneur with a vision to revolutionize the tech industry. His idealism was his rocket fuel, propelling him to launch a startup with a groundbreaking idea. However, Alex's journey wasn't smooth. His unwavering focus on his grand vision often clashed with the practical aspects of running a business. He faced tough choices, balancing his dreams with the hard truths of budget constraints, team limitations, and market demands. This struggle between idealism and realism became Alex's daily tightrope walk, teaching him valuable lessons about the essence of effective leadership.

CASE STUDY 1: THE HARMONY OF VISION AND REALITY

Consider the story of Sophia, CEO of an eco-friendly clothing brand. Sophia's idealism drove her to envision a world where fashion and sustainability coexist. However, she understood that this vision needed a realistic approach. By setting incremental, achievable goals and adapting to market trends, Sophia successfully balanced her idealistic aspirations with realistic strategies. Her brand gradually became a leader in sustainable fashion, proving that harmonizing dreams with practicality can lead to remarkable success.

CASE STUDY 2: THE PITFALL OF LOSING BALANCE

Contrastingly, there's the tale of Michael, a tech visionary whose idealism overshadowed realism. His ambition to create a groundbreaking product led him to ignore market research and team feedback. The result was a highly innovative but impractical product that failed to resonate with consumers. Michael's neglect of the realistic aspects of leadership and market demands led to a costly failure, highlighting the risks of an imbalanced approach.

Practical Tips: Walking the Leadership Tightrope

Regular Reality Checks: Regularly assess the feasibility of your goals against available resources and market conditions.

Open Communication: Foster an environment where team members can voice concerns and offer realistic insights.

Flexible Goal Setting: Set ambitious goals but be willing to adjust them based on practical considerations.

Celebrate Small Wins: Recognize and celebrate incremental achievements that contribute to your larger vision.

Continuous Learning: Stay informed about industry trends and be open to adapting your strategies accordingly.

REFLECTIVE QUESTIONS: SELF-ASSESSMENT ON THE LEADERSHIP SPECTRUM

Do I often find myself prioritizing ideals over practical considerations?

How do I react when faced with practical limitations to my vision?

Do I encourage open discussions about the feasibility of our goals?

How often do I adjust my strategies based on real-world feedback and results?

Am I able to find excitement and motivation in achieving smaller, realistic milestones?

In conclusion, the journey of leadership is a delicate dance between the stars of idealism and the gravity of realism. By mastering this balance, leaders can steer their teams toward success, ensuring that their visionary goals are grounded in the realities of the world they navigate.

As we conclude our exploration of balancing realism and idealism in leadership, it's beneficial to delve deeper into this topic. For those seeking to expand their understanding and skills in navigating this crucial aspect of leadership, here are three recommended readings. These resources offer valuable insights and practical advice, helping leaders to effectively bridge the gap between aspirational goals and practical realities.

"Good to Great: Why Some Companies Make the Leap and Others Don't" by Jim Collins

- Collins' book provides an in-depth analysis of how companies transition from being good to truly great. It emphasizes the importance of disciplined people, thought, and action in achieving extraordinary results. This book is particularly relevant for understanding how to balance ambitious visions with practical strategies.

"The Lean Startup: How Today's Entrepreneurs Use Continuous Innovation to Create Radically Successful Businesses" by Eric Ries

- Ries introduces a methodology that helps entrepreneurs and leaders develop their businesses and products efficiently. The book focuses on the concept of building-measure-learn feedback loops, which is essential for balancing idealistic innovation with realistic market testing.

"Mindset: The New Psychology of Success" by Carol S. Dweck

- Dweck's work explores the power of our mindset in achieving success. The book differentiates between fixed and growth mindsets, providing insights into how our beliefs about our abilities influence our behavior and success. It's a crucial read for leaders aiming to foster a balance between aspirational growth and realistic expectations.

As we move forward in our leadership journey, these readings can serve as a compass, guiding us in harmonizing our dreams with the realities of our environment. They offer a deeper dive into the art of leading with both vision and pragmatism, a skill essential for any leader aiming to make a lasting impact.

CHAPTER 10

Prioritizing Family in Leadership

*"Integrate your leadership with your life; a leader who values
family cultivates a team that respects humanity above all."*

In the heart of every leader's journey lies a fundamental truth often over-shadowed by the demands of success and the pursuit of professional fulfill-ment: the irreplaceable value of family. Chapter 10, "Prioritizing Family in Leadership," is an ode to the delicate yet powerful equilibrium between the rigor of leadership and the warmth of family life. It is a chapter that speaks to the soul of every leader who strives to weave the threads of career ambi-tion with the rich tapestry of personal life.

Imagine a world where the boardroom and the living room harmonize, where the lessons learned in leading teams resonate in nurturing a family, and where the strength drawn from a loving home empowers decisive and compassionate leadership. This is not a utopian dream but a practical real-ity that can be achieved through mindful balance and prioritization.

In this chapter, we explore the profound impact that prioritizing family has on a leader's effectiveness, resilience, and overall well-being. We delve into the stories of leaders who have navigated the tumultuous seas of corporate demands while anchoring themselves in the tranquility of family life. Their journeys illuminate the path for others, showcasing that true leadership success encompasses not just professional achievements, but also the joy and fulfillment found in family bonds.

We will uncover the strategies that successful leaders employ to maintain this balance, ensuring that their professional responsibilities do not overshadow the fundamental human need for connection, love, and belonging. This chapter is a testament to the fact that prioritizing family does not diminish a leader's impact; rather, it enriches it, providing a wellspring of support, perspective, and inspiration.

As we turn the pages of this chapter, let us embrace the idea that the heart of effective leadership beats not only in the halls of power but also in the comfort of home. The journey through "Prioritizing Family in Leadership" is not just about finding balance; it's about discovering a more fulfilling and sustainable way to lead, live, and love.

Anecdote: Balancing Family and Leadership - The Story of Dr. Maria Gonzalez

Dr. Maria Gonzalez, a director at a bustling city hospital, faced the formidable challenge of juggling her demanding career with her roles as a mother and wife. In a profession where emergencies are the norm and long hours are expected, Maria found herself constantly navigating the delicate balance between her professional responsibilities and her commitment to her family.

Despite the unpredictable nature of her job, Maria was determined to be an active presence in her family's life. She often woke up before dawn, a quiet time she used for planning her day or sometimes catching up on work, ensuring she could have breakfast with her children. These early morning moments were sacred to her, a time for bonding and connecting with her family before the day's chaos unfolded.

Maria's dedication to her family extended beyond mornings. She made it a rule to keep her weekends as free as possible for family time, except in the case of critical work emergencies. This commitment sometimes meant delegating responsibilities to her capable team or rearranging her schedule, but to Maria, it was a non-negotiable aspect of her life.

Her approach to balancing work and family was not without its challenges. There were days when emergencies at the hospital meant missing a family dinner or a school play. However, Maria's consistent effort to be there for the big moments - birthdays, anniversaries, and school events - built a foundation of trust and understanding with her family.

This commitment to her family did not go unnoticed. It fostered a deep sense of understanding and support from her husband and children, which in turn, gave her the emotional strength and peace of mind to tackle her professional responsibilities with vigor and enthusiasm. Maria's story is a testament to the fact that even in the most demanding careers, with thoughtful planning and clear priorities, it is possible to maintain a fulfilling family life alongside a successful professional journey.

CASE STUDY 1 (POSITIVE): THE STORY OF JAMES - A LEADER WHO PRIORITIZED FAMILY

James, the CEO of a rapidly expanding tech startup, held a firm belief that a successful career should not overshadow family life. He was a visionary leader, but for him, his family was the anchor that kept him grounded. James meticulously structured his work schedule to ensure he was home for dinner every night, a time he cherished for reconnecting with his family.

His commitment to family extended beyond just being physically present. He actively participated in his children's lives, attending school events, and ensuring he was there for bedtime stories, creating lasting memories and bonds. This balance between work and family life was not just a personal choice but a core value that James integrated into his company's culture.

Under his leadership, the company not only flourished in the competitive tech industry but also became known for its family-friendly policies. James introduced flexible working hours, remote working options, and parental leave policies that reflected his belief in the importance of work-life balance. This approach not only benefited his employees but also created a loyal and dedicated workforce.

James's balanced approach to leadership and family life provided him with a unique perspective. His decision-making was often more thoughtful and empathetic, considering the well-being of his employees alongside the company's objectives. His grounded approach led to innovative solutions and strategies, contributing to the company's success and reputation as a great place to work.

CASE STUDY 2 (NEGATIVE): THE DOWNFALL OF ALEX - NEGLECTING FAMILY

Alex's story is a cautionary tale of how neglecting family can lead to both personal and professional turmoil. As a high-flying executive in a leading multinational corporation, Alex was consumed by his ambition. His rapid ascent up the corporate ladder was fueled by long hours, relentless dedication, and frequent business travel.

However, this success came at a significant cost - his relationship with his family. Alex's intense focus on his career left little room for his spouse and children. Birthdays, anniversaries, and school events often went unattended, as work was always the priority. This constant absence created a growing rift between him and his family, leading to feelings of neglect and resentment.

The strain in his family life began to manifest in his professional life. The stress and guilt from his personal life started affecting his concentration, decision-making, and leadership style. His once sharp and charismatic demeanor began to wane, replaced by a distracted and often irritable presence.

The turning point came when Alex's personal life reached a crisis, forcing him to reevaluate his priorities. He realized that in his relentless pursuit of professional success, he had neglected the very foundation that supported him - his family. This realization was a wake-up call for Alex, but it came at a high cost. He understood that a successful career, devoid of personal fulfillment and family connections, was ultimately unfulfilling.

Both case studies highlight the critical importance of balancing professional ambitions with personal life, illustrating how prioritizing family can lead to a more fulfilling and sustainable career and life.

PRACTICAL TIPS FOR MAINTAINING A HEALTHY WORK-LIFE BALANCE

Set Boundaries: Define clear boundaries between work and family time. Avoid checking work emails or taking calls during family time unless it's an emergency.

Quality over Quantity: Make the most of the time you spend with family. Engage in activities that foster bonding and create lasting memories.

Flexible Scheduling: Whenever possible, adjust your work schedule to be present for important family events and milestones.

Delegate and Trust: Learn to delegate tasks at work. Trusting your team with responsibilities allows you to focus on family when you are away from work.

Self-Care: Remember that taking care of yourself is crucial. A well-rested and healthy leader is more effective both at work and home.

How often do I bring work stress into my family environment?

Am I present during family activities, or is my mind preoccupied with work?

Do I know the current interests and concerns of my family members?

How can I better integrate my work schedule with my family life?

What changes can I make to ensure I am there for my family's important moments?

These stories and tips highlight the importance of striking a balance between professional ambitions and personal life. They serve as a reminder that success in leadership is not just measured by professional achievements but also by the health and happiness of one's family life.

For those interested in delving deeper into the topic of work-life balance and family prioritization in leadership, as discussed in Chapter 10 of this book, here are three recommended readings that provide valuable insights and research findings:

"A Study on Moderating Role of Family-Friendly Policies in Work–Life Balance" by A. Nayak and Mrinalini Pandey. This study explores the relationship between work demand, work-family conflict, and the impact of family-friendly policies in reducing such conflicts. It's particularly insightful for understanding how organizational policies can support better work-life balance.

"Remote work and work-life balance: Lessons learned from the COVID-19 pandemic and suggestions for HRD practitioners" by

M. Shirmohammadi, Wee Chan Au, and Mina Beigi. This paper analyzes the challenges and lessons of remote work during the pandemic, offering insights into achieving work-life balance in a remote working environment.

"The impact of South African culture on the work-life balance of women in leadership positions" by Naong Matsidiso Nehemia and Naong Mammako Lenkoe. This research focuses on the challenges faced by women in leadership roles in balancing work and family life, particularly in the context of South African culture.

These resources offer a comprehensive view of the challenges and strategies related to maintaining a healthy balance between professional responsibilities and family life, especially for those in leadership positions. They provide both theoretical insights and practical advice, making them valuable additions to the exploration of this important topic.

CHAPTER 11

Going the Extra Mile: Beyond the Call of Duty

As I reflect on my journey as a leader, I'm struck by a profound realization: leadership is not just about fulfilling a role; it's about going the extra mile. It's about doing more than what's expected, more than what your team needs from you, and certainly more than what any job description could encapsulate. Let me share a story that encapsulates this lesson, a story that has become a cornerstone of my leadership philosophy.

It was a typical Monday morning, and I was preparing for the usual array of meetings and administrative tasks. But as I walked through the office, I noticed something unusual. There was a palpable sense of unease among my team. I could have easily ignored it, buried myself in my office, and focused on my agenda. But something inside me urged me to pause and pay attention.

I approached one of my team members, Sarah, and asked if everything was okay. She hesitated at first, but then shared that her father had been diagnosed with a serious illness. She was struggling to balance work and family commitments, and it was clearly taking a toll on her.

In that moment, I realized that my role as a leader extended far beyond strategizing and decision-making. It was about being there for my team, not just as a boss, but as a human being who cares. I reassured Sarah that she could take the time she needed to be with her family and that we would manage her workload in her absence.

But I didn't stop there. I organized a meeting with my team and openly discussed the importance of supporting each other, not just in our professional roles but in our personal challenges too. We brainstormed ways to improve our work-life balance and support mechanisms within the team.

This experience taught me a valuable lesson. Leadership is about going the extra mile. It's about recognizing that your team is made up of individuals with their own struggles and challenges. It's about understanding that sometimes, the most impactful thing you can do as a leader is to step out of your role and simply be there for someone in need.

From that day forward, I made a conscious effort to connect with my team on a deeper level, to understand their aspirations and fears, and to support them not just in achieving our organizational goals but in navigating the complexities of life. This approach not only strengthened our bond as a team but also led to increased trust, loyalty, and, ultimately, a more compassionate and effective leadership style.

In the end, going the extra mile as a leader has taught me that leadership is not just about what you accomplish, but about the impact you make on the lives of those you lead. It's about showing up, not just as a leader, but as a human being who cares deeply about the well-being of others. This, I believe, is the essence of true leadership.

As I reflect on the chapters of my leadership journey, I'm reminded of the countless moments where going the extra mile wasn't just a choice, but a calling. In the first chapter, I delved into the essence of trust. It wasn't merely about establishing trust; it was about nurturing it with every fiber of my being. I remember sharing stories with my team, transparently and consistently, even when times were tough. This approach wasn't born out of a manual; it stemmed from a deep-seated desire to create an environment brimming with genuine trust.

In the second chapter, the focus shifted to visionary leadership. Here, I didn't just set goals; I wove my team into the very fabric of our vision. It was a commitment to inclusivity, ensuring every voice was not just heard but valued. This wasn't a mandated strategy; it was a belief in the power of a shared, collective vision.

The art of effective communication was the crux of the third chapter. I aimed to transcend the norms of communication, striving for empathy and impact. Tailoring my approach to each team member's unique needs, I sought to forge connections that went beyond the superficial, driven by a heartfelt desire to truly understand and connect with my team.

Chapter four brought to light the role of empathy in leadership. Here, going the extra mile meant immersing myself in the perspectives of each team member, not just as their leader but as someone who genuinely cared. This wasn't about fulfilling an obligation; it was about leading with a heart full of empathy and understanding.

In the fifth chapter, the weight of decision-making was palpable. I often found myself spending extra hours pondering over decisions, not just their immediate impact but their ripples across the team. This meticulous approach was fueled by a personal ethic to make decisions that were best for everyone involved.

The sixth chapter was a delicate balance of trust and verification. Implementing systems to ensure accountability while fostering a culture of trust was a tightrope walk. This extra effort was a testament to my commitment to fairness and integrity.

Recognizing and navigating unseen influences was the focus of the seventh chapter. Here, I constantly educated myself, staying abreast of the subtle dynamics that influence leadership. This was driven by a dedication to being an informed and adaptive leader.

Chapter eight was about staying grounded. It was more than humility; it was about being deeply connected with my team's day-to-day realities. Sharing personal stories of involvement and awareness, I led not from a pedestal but from within the ranks.

In the ninth chapter, the challenge was balancing realism with idealism. I often found myself pushing boundaries to inspire my team while ensuring our goals remained grounded and achievable. This was driven by a desire to lead a team that was both motivated and realistic.

The tenth chapter brought into focus the importance of work-life balance. Prioritizing family was not just a chapter in a book; it was a chapter in my life. Actively making time for family and encouraging my team to do the same was a belief in the value of a fulfilling life beyond work.

In conclusion, my journey through these chapters was not a checklist of leadership duties. It was a manifestation of my internal compass, an unwavering commitment to do my best, and a personal desire to lead not just effectively, but with compassion and wholehearted dedication.

As you stand at the threshold of your leadership journey, you may find yourself navigating through a labyrinth of advice, theories, and strategies. In this sea of information, this book emerges not just as a guide, but as a companion, illuminating the path for new leaders like you. Here's why this book is an indispensable resource for your journey:

Real-Life Stories, Real Lessons: Unlike textbooks that offer theoretical knowledge, this book is steeped in real-life anecdotes and experiences. Each chapter unfolds a story, a lesson learned not in classrooms, but in the trenches of leadership. These stories resonate, teach, and inspire, offering you practical wisdom that you can apply in your own leadership journey.

Comprehensive Leadership Spectrum: From building trust to balancing work-life, this book covers the entire spectrum of leadership. It doesn't just focus on the conventional aspects like decision-making and communication but delves into often-overlooked areas like empathy, staying grounded, and the importance of family. This holistic approach ensures that you're well-equipped for diverse leadership challenges.

Personal and Relatable Tone: Written in a first-person narrative, the book speaks directly to you. It's like having a mentor who shares their journey, making the lessons more personal and relatable. This approach helps in internalizing the teachings, making them a part of your leadership ethos.

Practical Tips and Reflective Questions: Each chapter concludes with practical tips and reflective questions, turning theory into action. These sections encourage you to not just read but engage with the content, apply it in your context, and introspect, leading to deeper learning and self-awareness. Balancing Idealism and Realism: The book beautifully balances idealism and realism, a critical aspect for new leaders. It inspires you to dream big and pursue visionary goals while staying grounded in the practical realities of leadership. This balance is crucial for sustainable success and personal growth.

Emphasis on Going the Extra Mile: The book emphasizes the importance of going beyond the call of duty. It's about leading not because you have to, but because you want to. This perspective instills a sense of intrinsic motivation and passion for leadership, which is vital for new leaders.

Diverse Perspectives and Case Studies: With a range of case studies, both positive and negative, the book offers a 360-degree view of leadership. Understanding different scenarios and outcomes prepares you for real-world leadership challenges.

Recommended Readings and Resources: Each chapter provides additional resources for further exploration. This feature is invaluable for new leaders who wish to delve deeper into specific aspects of leadership. Accessible to a Wide Audience: The book is written in a style that is engaging and easy to understand, making it accessible to a wide audience. Whether you're a budding leader or someone with a bit of experience, the book speaks to you.

In essence, this book is not just about learning how to lead; it's about embarking on a journey of transformation. It's about shaping you into a leader who is not only effective but also empathetic, grounded, and balanced. As you turn each page, you'll find yourself growing, not just as a leader, but as a person, ready to take on the leadership world with confidence, compassion, and a deep understanding of what it truly means to lead.

IMPACTING LEADERSHIP

A Testament to Transformation

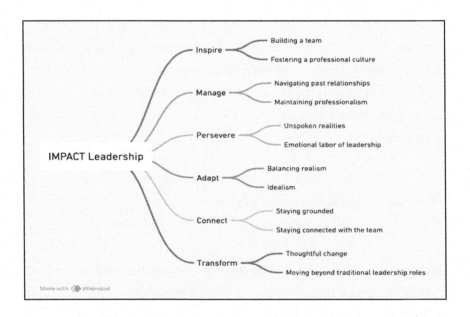

This book is more than just a collection of words and experiences; it's a testament to a transformative journey that has reshaped my life and, I hope, will touch yours too. As I penned down these pages, I delved deep into the reservoir of my life's experiences, each one a stepping stone that led me to where I stand today.

My journey began with a bold leap—leaving the familiar shores of St. Vincent and the Grenadines to embrace a new career in a foreign land. This leap was not just geographical; it was a leap of faith, a venture into the unknown, stepping out of my comfort zone into a world that was culturally alien and challenging. My career as a nurse was more than a profession; it was the crucible where my leadership was forged. In the corridors of healthcare, amidst the challenges of patient care in ICU, Telemetry, and Stepdown units, I learned the profound lesson of serving before leading.

Inspire: My tenure in the ICU taught me the power of inspiration. Early in my career, I faced an influx of critical cases, each presenting unique challenges. During this period, I convened a team meeting to share stories of resilience and recovery, aiming to reignite the passion and dedication of my team. This act of fostering hope and courage during adversity became a pivotal moment, enhancing our collective commitment to patient care. I learned that to truly inspire is to ignite the same passion in others that burns within you, especially when the stakes are high and the pressure is immense.

> *"True inspiration in leadership comes not from asserting authority, but from igniting the same fire in others that burns within you, especially when the night is darkest."*

Manage: In Telemetry, the essence of management became clear. Transitioning to a leadership role, I was responsible for a diverse team, requiring a sharp focus on maintaining seamless operations and high standards of patient care. Through a system of open communication and regular feedback, I optimized workflow, reduced errors, and significantly improved outcomes. My approach emphasized clarity and precision, ensuring that every team member understood their role and the overarching goals of our unit.

"Effective management isn't about overseeing people; it's about aligning souls towards a common vision with clarity and precision."

Persevere: The Stepdown unit was where perseverance became my mantra. Here, I navigated multifaceted challenges—from managing the complex needs of post-ICU patients to addressing staff burnout. I led by example, often extending my shifts to provide support during critical times, and advocated tirelessly for the resources needed to enhance both patient care and staff well-being. This resilience helped us overcome numerous obstacles and build a stronger, more dedicated team.

"Perseverance in leadership means standing firm in the storm, not because you will not waver, but because your resolve is the anchor for those you lead."

Adapt: Adaptability has been crucial throughout my leadership journey in healthcare, an ever-evolving field. Whether integrating new technologies or embracing innovative methodologies, I took the initiative to stay ahead of the curve, learning quickly and training my team effectively. This proactive approach not only kept us at the forefront of medical care but also underscored my commitment to innovation and continuous improvement.

"In the fluid dance of healthcare, the best leaders don't just embrace change; they lead the rhythm, making adaptability their most trusted partner."

Connect: Through my involvement in professional organizations like the American Nurses Association, I expanded my network, connecting with leaders and innovators across the field. These connections proved invaluable for sharing knowledge, collaborating on initiatives, and bringing best practices back to my teams. Building these relationships reinforced a culture of collaboration and mutual support in every setting I've worked in.

*"Leadership thrives on connection; it is the bridge built
not of stone, but of mutual respect and shared aspirations,
that carries us over the torrents of isolation."*

Transform: The most fulfilling aspect of my leadership has been the opportunity to transform both the environments I've worked in and the people I've worked with. By encouraging team members to pursue further education and take on new responsibilities, I've watched many evolve into leaders themselves. This focus on developing people's potential has not only enhanced our capabilities as a team but also ensured a legacy of skilled and compassionate care providers.

*"To transform is the essence of leadership. It is not about changing
what is, but unlocking what can be, in ourselves and in others."*

This book weaves these threads into a cohesive narrative, illustrating how these principles of IMPACT have guided me and defined the contours of effective leadership in nursing and beyond. Reflecting on my roots, I often think about my childhood in a neighborhood shadowed by adversity. Many of my friends from those days remain trapped in the same cycle of despair. Yet, whenever I return, I see a glimmer of pride in their eyes—a silent acknowledgment that if one of us succeeds, it's a victory for us all. This realization is a poignant reminder of the power of leadership and inspiration, even in the most unlikely places.

ACKNOWLEDGMENTS

As I reflect on the journey that led to the creation of this book, my heart is filled with gratitude for the myriad of individuals who have influenced, inspired, and shaped my understanding of leadership. This book is not just a product of my experiences and insights but a tapestry woven from the contributions of many remarkable individuals.

First and foremost, I extend my deepest appreciation to all the CEOs, Directors, and Managers I have had the privilege of working with and sitting on committees with. Your diverse perspectives, leadership styles, and professional ethics have immensely enriched my understanding of what it means to lead effectively and with integrity. Your willingness to share your experiences, both triumphs and challenges, has been invaluable.

To the leaders who have directly mentored me, your guidance has been a guiding light in my career. Your wisdom, patience, and unwavering support have not only shaped me as a professional but also as a person. You have shown me the power of mentorship in leadership, and for that, I am eternally grateful.

I also wish to acknowledge those leaders who, perhaps unknowingly, taught me what not to emulate. Your examples have been equally instructive, providing me with a clear understanding of the pitfalls and missteps in leadership. These lessons have been crucial in helping me shape my own leadership style – one that strives for empathy, integrity, and effectiveness.

A special thanks goes to my family and friends for their endless support and understanding. Balancing the demands of writing this book with personal commitments was not always easy, and your patience and encouragement have been the bedrock of my resilience and determination.

To my colleagues and peers in the industry, your insights and feedback have been instrumental in refining the concepts and ideas presented in this book. Your diverse viewpoints and experiences have added depth and richness to its pages.

Lastly, I extend my gratitude to the readers of this book – the aspiring, emerging, and established leaders who seek to make a positive impact in their spheres of influence. It is my sincere hope that the contents of this book will inspire you, challenge you, and equip you with the tools to lead with both confidence and humility.

This book is a tribute to all of you – the mentors, the colleagues, the challenging personalities, and the supporters. Thank you for being part of my journey and for contributing to the collective wisdom that this book represents.

With heartfelt thanks,

Earl Wilson